MOMENTS
OF
STRENGTH

MOMENTS
40 DAYS OF
INSPIRATION FOR MEN
OF
STRENGTH

TYNDALE
MOMENTUM

A Tyndale nonfiction imprint

Visit Tyndale online at tyndale.com.

Visit Tyndale Momentum online at tyndalemomentum.com.

Tyndale, Tyndale's quill logo, *Tyndale Momentum*, and the Tyndale
Momentum logo are registered trademarks of Tyndale House Ministries.
Tyndale Momentum is a nonfiction imprint of Tyndale House Publishers,
Carol Stream, Illinois.

Walk Thru the Bible and the Walk Thru the Bible logo are registered
trademarks of Walk Thru the Bible Ministries, Inc.

Moments of Strength: 40 Days of Inspiration for Men

Some of these devotions were previously published by Walk Thru the Bible
in the September 2013 issue of *Stand Firm* magazine.

For information about special discounts for bulk purchases, please
contact Tyndale House Publishers at csresponse@tyndale.com or call
1-855-277-9400.

ISBN 978-1-4964-5748-6

Printed in the United States of America

30	29	28	27	26	25	24
7	6	5	4	3	2	1

INTRODUCTION

As men, we often feel challenged to prove our worth to the people around us, whether it's at home (in our families), at work (as employees or supervisors), or with our friends. But with all the demands on our time, energy, and resources—not to mention our relationships—we can feel weak, overwhelmed, and exhausted. Thankfully, God never intended for us to go it alone, in our own power. He designed us to draw our strength and direction from Him, and to find encouragement and inspiration in community with our families and with other men. In fact, God tells us, "My grace is sufficient for you, for my power is perfected in weakness" (2 Corinthians 12:9, CSB) and "[we] can do everything through Christ, who gives [us] strength" (Philippians 4:13).

This book of devotions is an invitation for you to spend a few minutes in quiet conversation with God—whether it's first thing in the morning, during your lunch break, or just before bed. God designed us to function best (and be strongest) when we regularly take time to connect with Him through His Word and in prayer. As God told the Israelites, "Only in returning to me and resting in me will you be saved. In quietness and confidence is your strength" (Isaiah 30:15).

The *Moments of Strength* devotional can be your means of connecting with God in the time and space you have available. It will also serve as a reminder that all your strength comes from God, and that He uses His strength to work through your weaknesses to accomplish His purpose and plan on earth. Written from a variety of perspectives and in a variety of styles, these devotions will encourage you to place your trust in the hands of the all-powerful God of the universe, in whom is found all you need to live your life for Him.

You can use the Moment of Strength Scripture passage at the end of each reading to take a deeper look at what God's Word says about that day's topic, and to initiate a conversation with God about the situations and people you encounter in your day-to-day life.

This resource from Walk Thru the Bible is designed to inspire you to fully embrace your relationship with God and to walk in the strength of His love, mercy, and grace. For "His divine power has given us everything required for life and godliness through the knowledge of him who called us by his own glory and goodness" (2 Peter 1:3, csb).

THE POWER WITHIN

*By his divine power, God has given us
everything we need for living a godly life. We
have received all of this by coming to know
him, the one who called us to himself by
means of his marvelous glory and excellence.*

2 PETER 1:3

Living the Christian life isn't difficult — it's impossible! We learn what God desires, we strive to align our priorities with His will, we meet with other men to keep us on track, and still we stumble. Even Paul, as mature and sold out in his faith as he was, lamented the pull of sin in his life (Romans 7:15-24). Yet we have this promise from the apostle Peter that "God has given us everything we need for living a godly life." But what does that entail? Read more, memorize more, serve more, pray more? Is that what it takes?

The answer isn't found in our effort; it's found in our relationship with God, who has "called us to himself." When we accept Christ's gift of salvation, we receive the Holy Spirit into our hearts. This is the divine power we now have (Acts 1:8). How we nurture this new relationship will affect our growth in the Christian life. If we go back to our old ways, we'll get nowhere. If we try our best without God, we'll fail. But when we invest the effort to know God through study, prayer, and obedience, He does a transforming work in our minds that we can't do for ourselves. Our desires align with His (Romans 8:5), we make sound judgments (2 Timothy 1:7), and we better recognize His escape hatches when temptation strikes (1 Corinthians 10:13). Best of all, we experience real life. Not just survival—*life*! Growing, fruit-bearing, accomplishing-our-God-given-purpose kind of life!

BOTTOM LINE

God doesn't call us to be holy and then
leave us to flop and flail. He gives us His
Spirit to transform us into sin-resistant,
fruit-bearing men of purpose.

MOMENT OF STRENGTH

Zechariah 4:6

THE WISDOM OF MAN

*He showed me another vision. I saw
the Lord standing beside a wall that
had been built using a plumb line.*

AMOS 7:7

There are a lot of helpful Christian books available,
and we encourage you to read as many of them as
you can. A reliable Christian author can offer valu-
able insights about the life of faith that God can use
to help grow your faith.

But is there any danger in reading how other
men interpret and apply Scripture? Possibly. We
need to measure a man's words against the Word of
God, just as we would use the builder's plumb line,
mentioned by the prophet Amos, to build a wall.

In his classic *The Pursuit of God*, A. W. Tozer

uses a similar illustration from music. A piano tuner doesn't tune one piano to another piano, because differences in tone would still occur and both pianos would still be a little bit out of tune. Instead, he tunes each piano to a tuning fork—a reliable and consistent standard—and thus even a hundred pianos, all tuned to the same tuning fork, will be perfectly tuned to each other.

What can we learn from that example? When we read our favorite, trusted authors, we shouldn't automatically take their interpretation of Scripture as the final word on the subject. Rather, we must apply God's "tuning fork"—His inspired and holy Word—to find His truth, measuring all things against Scripture. At the same time, we should recognize that our own interpretations are fallible as well, and it is wise to prayerfully study the Bible with other Christians.

BOTTOM LINE

Read your favorite authors, but look up the Scriptures they cite and see whether their ideas line up clearly with the Word of God.

MOMENT OF STRENGTH

Amos 7:7-9

GOD IS GOOD

The LORD is good and does what is right;
he shows the proper path to those who go
astray. He leads the humble in doing right,
teaching them his way. The LORD leads with
unfailing love and faithfulness all who keep
his covenant and obey his demands.

PSALM 25:8-10

Many of us could pass a theology test about God's character, but there's a huge difference between knowing what we're supposed to believe about God and actually believing in Him at a true heart level. The true test of our faith is how it affects the way we live our lives, especially when things go wrong.

Psalm 25:8 declares in no uncertain terms that God "is good and does what is right." Do you believe that? Really believe it? Has anything ever happened in your life that has caused you to seriously doubt God's goodness? Sooner or later (and probably multiple times) most of us will be tested at this very point: Is the Lord good despite what has happened? The answer according to Scripture is yes. "All the LORD's ways show faithful love and truth" (Psalm 25:10, CSB).

Notice the connection between the first half of verse 8—"The LORD is good and does what is right"—and the second half: "He shows the proper path to those who go astray." Verse 9 adds, "He leads the humble in doing right, teaching them his way." The Lord's goodness is demonstrated in how He treats sinners—which is *well*. Moreover, He "leads with unfailing love and faithfulness all who keep his covenant and obey his demands." As creatures who still struggle with sin (and a lack of humility), we are not in a good position to judge God. We don't actually know what *good* is. Instead, we're told to trust God because *He* is good.

BOTTOM LINE

God's goodness cannot be rightly judged
by our circumstances, which aren't
always good. He is good no matter
how things look on the outside.

MOMENT OF STRENGTH

Psalm 119:68

KNOW YOUR NEIGHBOR

Do not seek revenge or bear a grudge against a fellow Israelite, but love your neighbor as yourself. I am the LORD.

LEVITICUS 19:18

The word *neighbor* is mentioned more than 130 times in the Bible. Among other things, we're told not to give false witness against our neighbors (Exodus 20:16) or covet our neighbor's house or wife (Deuteronomy 5:21), and we're instructed to build up our neighbors for their good (Romans 15:2) and love our neighbors as ourselves (Leviticus 19:18). That last one is probably the most famous. Jesus even used those words when He was asked about the greatest command in all of the Old Testament law (Matthew 22:39).

Yet despite the importance the Bible places on how we treat our neighbors, research shows that many of us don't really know our neighbors. How can we love our neighbors if we don't even know them?

The Bible describes a neighbor in broad terms—including people in need whom we come across—not just people who live on our street. When we concentrate on knowing and loving the people in our community, we, too, are blessed. Studies show that when we know our neighbors, we build a safer, stronger, healthier environment to live in. And the best part is that it doesn't take a lot of effort to get to know our neighbors. We just need to be friendly and say hello. Taking the initiative may stretch our comfort level a little, but it's the right thing to do. We may even make some new friends and find opportunities to share the gospel in the process.

BOTTOM LINE

Make an effort to get to know your neighbors better. It's not complicated; it just takes a little intentional effort.

MOMENT OF STRENGTH

Matthew 22:36-40

DON'T STRESS ABOUT IT

Peace I leave with you. My peace I give to
you. I do not give to you as the world gives.
Don't let your heart be troubled or fearful.

JOHN 14:27, CSB

Jack couldn't shake the feelings of lethargy. That
"afternoon drowsiness" now seemed to stretch from
morning till night. He didn't sleep well, and his
supervisor had started to notice that his production
at work had dropped off. Plus, he'd put on a few
pounds that he couldn't lose. Jack didn't know what
was wrong. *Maybe I should start taking vitamins or*
exercising more, he thought.

The real problem could have been stress. Stress
can manifest itself in a myriad of symptoms such
as the ones above or cause angry outbursts, sadness,

and irritability. Left unchecked, stress can lead to high blood pressure, heart disease, and diabetes.

All those symptoms may sound scary, especially since you can't always avoid stress. Life is filled with it: work deadlines, discipline issues with children, marital conflicts, and family issues. Though stress may be unavoidable, you can work with your doctor to make a plan to manage stress through physical activity, times of relaxation, and getting into God's Word. Plus, you have the ultimate stress buster in your life—the peace of the Lord.

In John 14:27, Jesus says, "I am leaving you with a gift—peace of mind and heart. And the peace I give is a gift the world cannot give. So don't be troubled or afraid." God doesn't want us to be overly stressed. Instead, He wants us to find our rest in Him.

BOTTOM LINE

Too much stress doesn't help anything.
If anything, it hurts us physically. Be
sure to schedule regular checkups with
your doctor. Seek to rest in God.

MOMENT OF STRENGTH

Matthew 11:28-29

SHARP AS A RAZOR'S EDGE

Using a dull ax requires great strength, so sharpen the blade.

ECCLESIASTES 10:10

An ax has to be sharpened often if its user is to experience its maximum utility. Whatever your occupation or hobby or interests, you know that your tools have to be maintained to get the best results. A knife must be sharpened. A uniform must be laundered. A motor must have oil, and a baseball glove must be oiled. Computer software has to be updated.

Whatever you're doing, the tools you're using have to be kept in prime condition if you expect to achieve the best results for the task at hand.

When it comes to a vibrant, effective Christian

faith, it's also imperative that your "tools" be sharp, always ready for whatever situation you face. If you want your faith to be strong, regularly sharpen the tools that make it possible. Some of those tools are study, prayer, fellowship, serving, and worship.

Spend time reading the Bible, participate with an accountability partner or a small group of men you trust, find ways to serve others selflessly (through your church or community groups), and never forget the critical role of worship in maintaining a strong faith. When, by the grace of God, you keep your faith tools sharp, you're well on your way to becoming a master faith builder. But if you don't, you may find your faith becoming less and less enjoyable and less and less effective. Build your faith to last.

BOTTOM LINE

Make a list of the faith tools you need
to sharpen, get out the sandpaper
or the file, and go to work.

MOMENT OF STRENGTH

Romans 12

SHARE EACH OTHER'S BURDENS

*Share each other's burdens, and
in this way obey the law of Christ.*

GALATIANS 6:2

Have you ever gone through such a difficult trial
that, if not for the help and encouragement of your
friends, you're not quite sure how you would have
made it through? The truth is, we need each other.
God designed the church to function as a family,
and members of a healthy family are there for each
other during the tough times.

Hebrews 3:13 tells us, "You must warn each
other every day, while it is still 'today,' so that none
of you will be deceived by sin and hardened against
God." There is a sense in which we *are* our brothers'

keepers. We are called to love and encourage one another daily. No man is an island, especially in the church. So when we see a brother in need, we're called to step up and help. And when we're hurting, we need to be humble enough to ask others for help and receive it.

In sharing each other's burdens, we're told, we "obey the law of Christ." Jesus is our example here. He is the ultimate burden carrier, as He has removed from us the burden of our sins and the burden of perfect obedience to God's law. He has set us free. But the freedom we have is meant to be used in the service of God and others. That's actually what true freedom is: the ability to love others as God loves us. And God has given us His Spirit to enable us to be burden carriers for others. By God's grace, live a life of love.

BOTTOM LINE

We're called to carry each other's
burdens. That's not always easy, but
following Christ means being willing to
make sacrifices for the good of others.

MOMENT OF STRENGTH

Galatians 6:1-10

STAND STRONG WITH BROTHERS

> *As iron sharpens iron, so*
> *a friend sharpens a friend.*
>
> PROVERBS 27:17

In the 1940s, Edward Flanagan, founder of Boys Town, came across a drawing of an older youth carrying a younger boy on his back. The caption read, "He ain't heavy, he's my brother." Flanagan thought that it so perfectly illustrated what his ministry did that he commissioned a sculpture of the drawing that still stands on the Boys Town campus in Omaha.

In 1969, songwriters Bobby Scott and Bob Russell turned the phrase into a popular ballad, and the Hollies turned "He Ain't Heavy, He's My Brother" into a big hit.

As brothers in Christ, it is important that we encourage one another, challenge one another, and help one another stand strong when the ways of the world counter our faith. How do we do that? One way is to make ourselves accountable to a friend or a small group and to have appointed times—weekly is a good plan—when we ask each other hard questions. Some examples: *How much time have you spent studying the Bible this week? In prayer? How have you treated your wife this week? (Would she answer this question the same way?) What have you said or done this week for which you need to apologize? What are you believing about God right now? What are you believing about yourself?* It may not be easy to answer these kinds of questions, but it's worth the effort.

BOTTOM LINE

Find a brother or two who will meet with you weekly—and agree never to shy away from the hard questions. Sharpen each other as followers of Jesus.

MOMENT OF STRENGTH

1 Thessalonians 3:6-13

LOOK AROUND

As I looked and thought about it,
I learned this lesson.

Many coaches like to use the phrase "teachable moment" for those times when players can learn from their stumbles. Maybe they went one way on the field of play when they should've gone the other. When that happens, there's an opportunity to learn and improve the next time around—to check out the playbook. It's all there in black and white.

The same thing goes for our lives as Christians. Every day, there are countless teachable moments all around us. Maybe it's the tone of voice you use with your wife and kids. Maybe it's the curse word that slips out when you're frustrated. Maybe it's making the same mistakes that so many others have made.

The context for today's verse is a walk past the field of a lazy person, which is "overgrown with nettles" and "covered with weeds" and has walls that "were broken down" (Proverbs 24:30-31). But the lesson to be learned can also apply to many other situations.

See, and take it to heart. Look, and receive instruction!

We have an infinite number of ways to appreciate God and learn from Him. Some lessons are harder to understand and apply to our lives than others. Some might require us to do our homework again until we get it just right. But don't worry. God's patience is infinite. He is the ultimate teacher.

BOTTOM LINE

Pray for God's strength to take
teachable moments and apply them
to your daily walk with Him.

MOMENT OF STRENGTH

Proverbs 3.13

WHAT ARE YOU CULTIVATING?

*As he scattered it across his field, some of
the seed fell on a footpath, and the birds
came and ate it. Other seed fell on shallow
soil with underlying rock. The seed sprouted
quickly because the soil was shallow.*

MARK 4:4-5

We live in a generation that, for the most part,
knows little about farming and agriculture, though
we are heavily dependent on those who work the
land. But since we know so little of the process, it
is not unusual that we may sometimes misuse com-
mon terms that relate to farming.

We may hear people talk about cultivating crops.
But the soil itself is what is cultivated, both in pre-
paration for planting crops and in tending the crops
as they grow. In a sermon at the Francis Asbury
Society's 2011 fall conference, seminary professor

Dr. Victor Hamilton made the point that we cultivate the soil, not the crop. Dr. Hamilton then drew a spiritual parallel—we cultivate our hearts, preparing them to receive the seed of God's Word. We then continue to cultivate the heart, allowing the Word to grow and thrive.

To keep our hearts prepared for God's Word to grow requires a few basic things. The first is *desire*. If we don't want the Word of God in our hearts, it won't be there. Everything starts with desire. Second, we prepare our hearts by *studying the Bible*. And third, we prepare by communicating regularly with God through *prayer* and in *worship*. Only as these elements come together in our hearts will we have hearts where His truth can grow.

BOTTOM LINE

Cultivating the soil of your heart to make it more fertile for God's Word is an ongoing challenge and a great blessing.

MOMENT OF STRENGTH

Psalm 51:10-13

TAKING TIME TO REST

*This is what the Sovereign LORD, the Holy
One of Israel, says: "Only in returning to
me and resting in me will you be saved. In
quietness and confidence is your strength.
But you would have none of it."*

ISAIAH 30:15

With a myriad of activities and responsibilities fighting for our time and attention, it's often difficult to get everything done. There always seems to be more to do and less time to do it. Without enough time to complete everything, it becomes even more of a challenge to find the time for the rest we desperately need in order to function at peak performance.

According to the prophet Isaiah, our strength is closely tied to rest. In our busy culture, it's easy to think that rest is synonymous with laziness, but it's not. Rest is a disposition of the soul that flows out of a deep trust that God is in control and taking care of us. If we're honest with ourselves, we recognize that much of our busyness may be a result of insecurity about our standing with God. We try to silence our noisy consciences with activity.

You've no doubt heard it said that we are human *beings*, not human *doings*. Still, as men, it's easy for us to define ourselves by what we do and to quickly lose sight of who we are (apart from what we do). Rather than resorting to more activity as a means of dealing with the noise inside us, we should understand that God desires for us to *stop* and *rest* instead. In this stillness, God exposes our desire for self-sufficiency and reminds us that His love for us is based on who we are and not what we do. Don't you long for that? Don't you long for the "green pastures" and "quiet waters" of Psalm 23 (csb)? They are available for us.

BOTTOM LINE

If we think we need to earn anything
in our relationship with God, we will
live restless lives. What will you
do today to intentionally rest?

MOMENT OF STRENGTH

Luke 10:38-42

DISTRACTIONS

*Therefore, since we also have such a
large cloud of witnesses surrounding us,
let us lay aside every hindrance and the sin
that so easily ensnares us. Let us run with
endurance the race that lies before us.*

HEBREWS 12:1, CSB

Have you ever seen a group of people sitting at the
same table in a restaurant, and everyone is busy on
their smartphones? What's so important that they're
all practically ignoring each other? Is it possible
they're tweeting or updating their statuses about how
they're out with their friends? Come on. Put the
phones down!

Attention spans aren't what they used to be.
Before cable and satellite television, we were stuck
with basically three channels. Now, there are hundreds of channels. Don't like what you see when

you land on one? Change the channel. Change it again. And again. Let's not even begin to talk about the internet and how it can . . . oops, wait a second, there's an email coming in!

Life is crazy enough without all these other distractions. You've got plenty of family obligations, and your job keeps you busy enough. You're thankful for your wife, your kids, your job, and everything else, but those relationships and your job require time and care.

As easy as it is to get sidetracked these days, the one constant has to be Jesus. Consider how much time you spend on social media, the internet, TV, and whatever else you have going, and then think about how much time you spend with Jesus. No matter what else you've got on your mind, stay focused on Him.

BOTTOM LINE

Distractions are all around us. Keep
them in their rightful place, and focus
on your relationship with Jesus.

MOMENT OF STRENGTH

1 Corinthians 9:24-27

A GOD ENCOUNTER

[Jacob] reached a certain place and spent the night there because the sun had set. He took one of the stones from the place, put it there at his head, and lay down in that place.

GENESIS 28:11, CSB

Walking across the university graduation stage. Standing at the church altar on your wedding day. Pacing in a hospital birthing suite. Receiving a court summons. Strolling a Maui beach. Waiting in an emergency room. Looking down at a loved one in a casket. Certain places have significant meaning. In fact, certain sights, certain smells, or even a glimpse of someone who looks familiar can flood our minds with memories and escalate our emotions. Some of the events we recall are filled with great happiness and others with profound sorrow. Yet each holds a special place in our hearts.

In Genesis 28:11, we are told that Jacob reached "a certain place." The underlying Hebrew phrase may simply describe a locale, but it often refers to a sanctuary. This "certain place" was a particular sacred spot—a transforming place—and it was sacred because God was there. Jacob was not expecting to see God in this place, but he did.

God is not absent. He is involved and at work in our lives. If we are His children, we can be certain that He hasn't forgotten us. Just because we may not see what He is doing doesn't mean He isn't doing anything. God often works behind the scenes and in ways we will never know on this side of eternity. Are you awake to His presence and activity?

BOTTOM LINE

God doesn't always change the
circumstances of our lives, but He can use
our circumstances to change us. If we look
and listen, we just might encounter God.

MOMENT OF STRENGTH

Psalm 59:10

FLEXIBLE FAITH

If you had faith even as small as a mustard seed, you could say to this mountain, "Move from here to there," and it would move. Nothing would be impossible.

MATTHEW 17:20

Have you ever had big plans with a lot of details that had to fall into place with perfect timing? Maybe it was when you built the shop in the backyard. There wasn't much extra space, so everything needed to be delivered in the right order. The concrete truck had to be able to turn around in the backyard without piles of building supplies in the way.

Next, you wanted the lumber to frame up the building, then shingles for the roof. And you really didn't want all the stuff for finishing the inside—drywall, paint, electrical, plumbing—until you were ready to use it.

But the building supply company brought the shingles early and left them right where the concrete truck would need to turn around. Then a huge box of light fixtures, switches, and wiring that you'd ordered online was the second item to arrive. Suddenly, you had to adapt and go to plan B.

Sometimes, faith is like that—we're praying, working toward a goal, and even trusting God to make things happen the way we think they ought to. But we have to learn to be flexible when God works in unexpected ways and to be grateful for however He responds to our faith. As we live by faith, we move ahead by God's timetable, not ours. And we experience a lot more peace when we don't try to control everything, but instead leave it up to God.

BOTTOM LINE

Learning to be flexible will strengthen
your faith and help you cultivate patience
and gratitude. Is there an area in your life
right now that needs this approach?

MOMENT OF STRENGTH

Galatians 2:19-21

THE RIGHT ATTITUDE

Do everything without grumbling and arguing, so that you may be blameless and pure, children of God who are faultless in a crooked and perverted generation, among whom you shine like stars in the world.

PHILIPPIANS 2:14-15, CSB

It's easy to find things wrong with the world. You don't have to go too far to discover imperfection and inconvenience. Even though you could complain about these things, should you? For example, during a quick drive in the car, there are red lights, traffic slowdowns, fast drivers, slow drivers, and drivers who cut you off, and the list goes on. But because God has different standards for His people than what's "normal" or "reasonable," it is possible for us as believers to "shine like stars in the world." This may seem grandiose at first, but a person who takes things in stride without complaining is a rare breed.

On what basis should a Christian not complain? What makes us different from the world? We know our heavenly Father is in control of all things. We know that some of the inconveniences we experience may actually be divine opportunities to help someone else, or for God to grow us. Either way, complaining doesn't honor God.

As Christians, we can rest in the fact that our Father is in charge. He's got us. We can be blameless, pure, and childlike. We don't have to worry and fret and try to control the outcome of everything, getting upset when things don't go our way. Not only does this kind of relaxed trust in God honor Him, but it makes our lives so much more attractive to others and enjoyable to ourselves.

BOTTOM LINE

Living a complaint-free life is a much happier and holier way to live. Besides, complaining never makes things better.

MOMENT OF STRENGTH

Numbers 11:1

WHAT'S PAST IS PAST

Do not remember the rebellious sins of my youth. Remember me in the light of your unfailing love, for you are merciful, O LORD.

PSALM 25:7

It wasn't exactly a weekly thing, but the Knight family routinely had the trees in their front yard rolled with toilet paper by a family friend. His efforts were works of art, if he did say so himself: roll after roll after roll hanging from the limbs, blowing in the breeze, and getting soggy in the rain. Many times, the culprit would help clean it all up.

Fast-forward twenty-five years or so. Now an adult, the former "yard artist" stayed with the Knight family during a visit to town. When he got to his room, it was completely covered with toilet paper.

The bed. The pillows. Hanging from light fixtures. Everywhere! It was sweet revenge for the Knights.

The Knights and their friend were able to laugh about the foolish stuff he had done as a teenager, but many people aren't that fortunate. Some kids get into more serious trouble and then spend much of their lives living it down—legally, emotionally, or both. Worst of all can be the guilt. Some people have a hard time experiencing God's forgiveness for the things they did, even though His forgiveness is available to them.

A life of faith is not about feeling guilty about things in your past. God's grace and forgiveness can give you a fresh start. The Cross is not for perfect people; it's for people who aren't perfect and who desperately need forgiveness. So don't believe the enemy's accusations. You are forgiven in Christ.

BOTTOM LINE

You might have messed up big time
as a kid or even as an adult, but God's
forgiveness is big enough to handle it. Let
His grace set you free from your past.

MOMENT OF STRENGTH

Psalm 103:12

TRUST FACTOR

*This I declare about the LORD: He
alone is my refuge, my place of safety;
he is my God, and I trust him.*

PSALM 91:2

How did I let him talk me into this? Richard wondered as he and his son, Josh, slowly rose into the air. The theme park they had visited the day before had been fun, but now Richard found himself strapped to Josh on the world's tallest Skycoaster.

"Are you sure we're just three hundred feet up?" Richard asked. "This feels way higher than a football field."

"Don't be a baby, Dad," Josh said. "It'll be fun."

Richard looked at the steel cable that suspended

them above the ground. *Okay*, he thought, *my life depends on the strength of that cable.*

Suddenly, Richard found himself speeding toward the ground at more than 70 mph. He was scared, but his fear couldn't wipe the smile off his face.

"This is awesome!" he shouted as they flew back in the other direction.

As Christians, we're supposed to trust Jesus with our lives. But our actions don't always show it. We may use words like the ones David uses in Psalm 91, but then we don't put our faith into action like David did.

Richard and Josh couldn't soar until they trusted the steel cable. It's much the same way in our Christian lives. We're stuck going nowhere until we trust Jesus to hold us up. Is there something you've wanted to do for God but were too afraid to try? Trust Him. Ask Him to increase your faith. He's way more reliable than any steel cable.

BOTTOM LINE

What's holding you back from stepping out for Jesus? Take a risk and discover the adventure that awaits.

MOMENT OF STRENGTH

Isaiah 12:2

FROM PRIDE TO THE PIT

*We were out in the field, tying up
bundles of grain. Suddenly my bundle
stood up, and your bundles all gathered
around and bowed low before mine!*

GENESIS 37:7

Joseph was one of the Bible's most memorable men.
Jacob had twelve sons, but he loved Joseph more
than the others (Genesis 37:3). And as expected,
such obvious parental favoritism did not play well
with the older brothers. Let's recall some of the
story's details.

First, Jacob dressed Joseph better than he clothed
the older brothers—Joseph's colorful coat contrasted
with the brothers' plain, drab robes (Genesis 37:3).
Earlier, Joseph had come home from tending sheep
and tattled on two of his brothers. Finally, we're told

that his brothers hated him and wouldn't even speak to him decently (Genesis 37:4).

When he was seventeen, Joseph boasted about a dream he had in which his brothers symbolically bowed down to him (Genesis 37:6-7). Did he really think this would endear him to them? Was he trying to prove that God was on his side? Not long after this dream, Joseph's brothers threw him into a pit and debated about killing him, but instead, they sold him into slavery (Genesis 37:26-28).

The evidence suggests that Joseph may have been an overly confident teenager. Fortunately, we have the rest of the story: He grew into a godly man of wisdom, integrity, forgiveness, compassion, and humility. Take time now to consider how these godly characteristics are reflected in your own life.

BOTTOM LINE

One of the keys to growing in godliness is spending more time focusing on God than on ourselves. Even so, sometimes an honest self-evaluation is helpful.

MOMENT OF STRENGTH

Genesis 37:1-11

SEEING THINGS ARIGHT

Joseph replied, "Don't be afraid of me. Am I God, that I can punish you? You intended to harm me, but God intended it all for good. He brought me to this position so I could save the lives of many people."

GENESIS 50:19-20

Joseph's brothers resented him because their father treated him specially. So when the opportunity presented itself, Joseph's brothers got rid of him—they sold him into slavery. It's hard for us to grasp, but they placed little value on human life, even the life of their own brother.

Years later, when the brothers had to go to Joseph for food during a great famine, they were terrified that he would want revenge. They remembered how badly they had treated him and how they had lied to their father. But despite the painful journey it took to get to that point, Joseph could see God's hand in all that had happened, and he wasn't bitter or vengeful.

Our perspective is often skewed by what we consider most important to us at the moment. If Joseph had viewed revenge against his brothers as most important, he would have reacted differently, and he likely would have missed the big picture of what God was doing through him. Like Joseph, we need to always remember the sovereignty of God. He is in control, and He is good. That's the right perspective to have.

When facing a troubling situation, try to look at the circumstances with eyes of faith—maybe a redemptive outcome will emerge from a seemingly bad situation. God is able to bring good out of bad in ways we never could have imagined.

BOTTOM LINE

God is up to good—we can be sure of
that. Trust Him to work things out in the
best possible way, in His perfect timing.

MOMENT OF STRENGTH

Genesis 50:15 21

LIVE LIKE A MOVIE TRAILER

We are Christ's ambassadors; God is making
his appeal through us. We speak for Christ
when we plead, "Come back to God!"

2 CORINTHIANS 5:20

What's the best part of going to the movies? For many of us, the trailers before the featured attraction create the most excitement. Making intriguing movie trailers is big business. Production companies are paid millions of dollars to choose the right music and pick the right scenes, so that after just a few minutes we think, *Wow, I want to see that!* Our first impression of a movie, based on the trailer, is often the deciding factor for whether we'll go see it.

As Christians, we should live our lives like a movie trailer. When people look at us, they should want to see the "rest of the show" and get to know Jesus personally. Second Corinthians 5:20 reminds us that "we are Christ's ambassadors." God makes His appeal through us. What an amazing thought. And what an awesome responsibility we have to encourage others to be reconciled to God.

Our words and actions should attract people to our Lord, not turn them off. As Christ's ambassadors, we must appeal to people and help draw them into God's theater. And unlike many Hollywood features that turn out to be disappointing, Jesus never does. With God, the real show is far better than the trailer. Though trailers often contain the best scenes and funniest lines, God's movie is compelling from beginning to end as it tells the greatest story ever told: the story of Jesus.

BOTTOM LINE

Does your life draw people to God's main attraction? Do they want to know Jesus because of you?

MOMENT OF STRENGTH

Ephesians 6:20

DAY 21

NOT A BIG DEAL

*The person who keeps all of the laws
except one is as guilty as a person
who has broken all of God's laws.*

JAMES 2:10

Big sins usually grow out of small sins. A movie
here, a website there, an inappropriate joke, fudging
the numbers—our choices may seem harmless at the
time, but they create a pattern, a slippery slope, and
sin tends to escalate over time. Too often, we lose the
battle against sin from the start because we under-
estimate its danger and damage. We let little things
creep up, and we make excuses such as "It's not that
big a deal." Before long, our spiritual vision can
become blurred so that we don't recognize sin as sin.

The truth is, every sin—even a small one—is

dangerous. Simple math reveals that if, instead of walking a perfectly straight line, you stray a mere one inch for every ten feet of travel and continue on that course for a day's walk, you'll wind up about a quarter mile from your intended destination. And that's just one day's walk. Continue on that path day after day and you'll find yourself in a different state, not just a different zip code.

The point is, excusing or failing to deal with sin can establish patterns that become destructive. Not only does it affect our character and our witness, it creates a barrier between us and God. Right now, prayerfully ask God to show you where you're stepping off His path, and then take the courageous step of committing, with His help, to walk the path of obedience.

BOTTOM LINE

Small compromises can be as dangerous
as blatant sins because they can go
unnoticed. Don't miss the opportunity
to make adjustments while you can.

MOMENT OF STRENGTH
Proverbs 3:6

THE PRIVILEGE OF PRAYER

Never stop praying.

1 THESSALONIANS 5:17

Prayer may be one of the biggest challenges Christian men face. Our world demands that we be constantly busy. We scarcely have time for quiet hours of thinking, meditation, or talking to God. We don't have time to sit on the front porch swing and reflect on life. We may not even have a front porch—much less a swing!

Still, the Bible clearly commands us to pray— and not just to pray, but to pray constantly. So let's resolve to start doing it. First, make a list of people and situations you could pray about: your family, a buddy who lost his job, the family whose home is being repossessed, your pastor and church, your workplace, a family friend with cancer, world and national affairs, your local community, or your doctor. The list can get long very quickly.

There are at least a couple of different ways to approach prayer. First, pray as a part of whatever you're doing. Pray while you're driving, working, exercising, doing yard work, etc. It takes only a few seconds to say a quick prayer before and during any activity.

Second, set aside time for focused prayer. Be intentional and consistent with this dedicated prayer time. There's no substitute for spending time with God. Practiced together, these two approaches can greatly improve your prayer life and intimacy with God.

BOTTOM LINE

Make sure that you're intentionally
cultivating your prayer life.
It's a great privilege!

MOMENT OF STRENGTH

Matthew 6:5-13

SIMPLE KINDNESS

*The generous will prosper; those who refresh
others will themselves be refreshed.*

PROVERBS 11:25

There are as many ways to show simple kindnesses as
there are stars in the sky. A soldier and his mother are
behind you in line for the cashier at the restaurant,
and when they get to the cashier, you've already taken
care of their bill. In the parking lot of the grocery
store, you offer to take an elderly lady's cart back
inside. You decide to visit a fellow church member
who's been going through a rough spell. You have a
basketful of groceries, and you allow someone with
a carton of milk to go ahead of you in line. It can be
as simple as holding a door open for someone.

Kindness doesn't have to be a major production. More often than not, there's no need for planning, strategy, or committee meetings. Some of the most sincere kindnesses take place on the spur of the moment. You see a chance to do something nice, and you take it! Pray that the Holy Spirit will give you eyes to see, and He will. Kindness and goodness are part of the fruit of the Spirit (Galatians 5:22-23).

The key here is simple. It may be easy to put money in the offering plate on Sunday, but it's the attitude behind the gift that's truly important. A truly generous heart seeks to do for others without any desire for recognition whatsoever, and it's not just a once-in-a-while thing, either. It's 24/7/365.

BOTTOM LINE

Whether the kindness is big or small,
it's the heart behind it that truly counts.

MOMENT OF STRENGTH

2 Corinthians 9:6-8

CONSIDER THE CONSEQUENCES

*In the end she's as bitter as wormwood
and as sharp as a double-edged
sword. Her feet go down to death;
her steps head straight for Sheol.*

PROVERBS 5:4-5, CSB

After a Christian leader had an affair, he said: "If only I had considered the cost this relationship would have on my family, my career, my witness, and my reputation, I would not have done it."

Perhaps before you venture down that same path, you should stop and weigh the long-term penalties. Adultery tries to cancel tomorrow's consequences by emphasizing today's delights. But it always costs more than you think. Adultery demands a toll, and the price is high.

Adultery will cost you your closest relationships.

Consider the hurt and pain it will inflict on your wife and family. It will also hurt your relationship with God. Adultery can cost you your strength. You will end up weak and worn out through your deceit and cover-ups. Adultery may cost you your money. You could end up spending a great deal of money on legal expenses if your marriage ends in divorce. Adultery can negatively affect your health. Long before people heard of chlamydia, syphilis, hepatitis, HIV, or AIDS, Solomon warned that those who commit adultery experience consequences "as bitter as wormwood." Adultery will cost you your reputation and destroy your Christian witness. You will lose respect and trust. In the end your sin will find you out. Minutes of gratification can cause a lifetime of pain.

BOTTOM LINE

Before you cross the line into sin, weigh the cost—and then don't cross the line!

MOMENT OF STRENGTH

Proverbs 6:27-29

THE SHOW

*Always be full of joy in the Lord.
I say it again—rejoice!*

PHILIPPIANS 4:4

It's the thick of the baseball season, and the pennant races are beginning to heat up. Soon, players in the minors will be called up to the big leagues, many for the very first time. Can you imagine what that moment must be like, when they get the news that they're going to the Show? They've worked a long time for this, and now it's actually happening.

Not everyone gets to play professional baseball, but joy and satisfaction come in pursuing countless other goals. Maybe you've always wanted to be a writer and you finally get an article published.

Or a promotion finally comes through at work. Or you want to get in better shape, and your waistline slowly but surely begins to shrink.

Most people have some sort of lifelong dream, and many may even get to experience theirs. Yet those pursuits pale in comparison to the day we'll achieve our ultimate prize—the day we're called home to heaven. Spending eternity with Jesus is so unimaginably wonderful that it's hard to comprehend it.

Revelation 21:4 promises a day when God "will wipe every tear from their eyes, and there will be no more death or sorrow or crying or pain. All these things are gone forever." What else could anyone ever want? Thank God for the gift of salvation that will allow you to spend eternity with Him.

BOTTOM LINE

Many people get to live out their
lifelong dreams, but we all have the
opportunity to land the ultimate prize—
life with Jesus in heaven. Praise God!

MOMENT OF STRENGTH

Revelation 5:9-13

GIVE TILL IT HURTS

Remember this—a farmer who plants only a few seeds will get a small crop. But the one who plants generously will get a generous crop.

2 CORINTHIANS 9:6

When it comes to giving financially to God's work, we've all heard the story of the poor widow who dropped two tiny coins into the Temple treasury. Jesus saw this and told His disciples that she had given more than anybody. "They have given a tiny part of their surplus, but she, poor as she is, has given everything she has" (Luke 21:4). That kind of generosity is rare. Were it not for Jesus holding her up as an example, we'd probably call her foolish for not taking care of herself first.

The widow gave until it hurt. That's a high

standard to strive to attain. The widow's two coins have proven mighty over the last couple of millennia as an example of sacrificial giving.

Today, studies show that people continue to give sacrificially. Those who can least afford it often give the highest percentage of their income.

No matter how much you've given or haven't given in the past, make it a priority, starting today, to give back to God in a way that honors Him. As God blesses us, we need to remember to bless others. The apostle Paul reminds us in 2 Corinthians 9:6 that "a farmer who plants only a few seeds will get a small crop. But the one who plants generously will get a generous crop." When we give generously to God, He can bring in a huge harvest that benefits us and others far beyond the accumulation of more money.

BOTTOM LINE

Prayerfully look for specific ways
to give this year that will have the
greatest impact for God's Kingdom.

MOMENT OF STRENGTH

Acts 20:35

A TIME AND A PLACE FOR YOU

From one man he created all the nations
throughout the whole earth. He decided
beforehand when they should rise and fall,
and he determined their boundaries.

ACTS 17:26

Do you ever wonder how you got to where you are?
For many of us, where we are now is nowhere near
where we thought we would be geographically, rela-
tionally, professionally, or spiritually. Rarely does life
go as planned. The truth is, we are not ultimately
the masters of our own fate—as popular as that idea
may be. ("If you can dream it, you can achieve it" is
not always true.)

In light of the winding, unpredictable road
you may have traveled thus far, does your life ever
seem random, maybe even purposeless? How do

you respond to that feeling? Do you decide to quit dreaming and planning? Or dismiss the idea that God created you for a purpose and may have you precisely where He wants you, despite all your sins, mistakes, and bad decisions? Giving in to doubt and despair is the kind of resignation that destroys hope and further clouds your purpose.

Part of the problem is that we often forget that our main purpose is to know God. "This is the way to have eternal life—to know you, the only true God, and Jesus Christ, the one you sent to earth" (John 17:3). When we're overly concerned with seeing our own plans come to fruition, we forget that knowing and loving God is what life is all about. When we get that right, everything else begins to make more sense. We start to see that every part of our journey is necessary, and that God can tell a good story with our lives despite the confusing parts.

BOTTOM LINE

Your life is not random. God is
weaving together a great story with
your life. Your job is to trust Him
and embrace the adventure.

MOMENT OF STRENGTH

Acts 17:27-28

THE POWER OF REASON

Avoiding a fight is a mark of honor;
only fools insist on quarreling.

PROVERBS 20:3

A company was converting to a group medical plan that required 100 percent participation. Everyone signed up, except for one employee. He refused. His friends and coworkers tried to convince him to sign up, but to no avail. Finally, his boss visited him and told him either to sign up or be fired. He signed up. His friends asked him what made the difference. He replied, "The boss explained it in a way I could understand."

Solomon reminded us that honor exists in doing what is right. Anyone can take the path of least resistance. Anyone can give in to pressure. It takes a strong person to make the difficult choice and come to the right decision.

Studies have shown that an immediate health effect will make more people change a habit than some distant threat. In other words, the more real and pressing the consequences, the greater the chance of change. That's why when confronted with the reality of death, people will stop smoking, lose weight, and start exercising.

Our bad habits, though often pleasurable, may be the reason we are not achieving the results we long for. We need a strong reason like health, success, better relationships, and, most important, the glory of God to ditch a bad habit.

Let the hope of a better future motivate you.

BOTTOM LINE

Are the things you're doing leading you to where you want to go? What do you need to change? Where do you need to look for motivation?

MOMENT OF STRENGTH

Proverbs 3:1-2

BARELY LIVING

*When Jesus saw him and knew he
had been ill for a long time, he asked
him, "Would you like to get well?"*

JOHN 5:6

The man in John 5 who had been an invalid for
thirty-eight years was alive, no doubt, but you might
argue whether he was really living. Not only was
he sick, but he also didn't have any friends to help
him (John 5:7). Finding the man in this state, Jesus
asked him what might seem to be an obvious question: "Would you like to get well?" Notice that Jesus
asked whether the man wanted to *get* well rather
than *be* well. Jesus healed the man immediately (so
he could be well physically), but His greater concern
was for the man's spiritual condition. That's why

Jesus sought the man out later and found him in the Temple. We read there that Jesus addressed the man's sin problem so that he could get well spiritually.

Don't misunderstand—we don't earn our salvation. If we could reconcile ourselves to God on our own, it wouldn't have been necessary for Jesus to leave His home in heaven the first time. But we can't, so He came, and now we have a choice of how to live. If you've been feeling down-and-out, by God's grace it's time to get up. He provides everything we need to be free of what holds us in bondage. Picking up your mat means taking responsibility for your life and working to remove those things in your life that have crippled you spiritually. It also means walking with God again in the freedom and power that He provides.

BOTTOM LINE

Don't settle for barely being alive
when God's will for you is to thrive
abundantly in the new life you have in
Christ. What's holding you back?

MOMENT OF STRENGTH

John 10:10

LEAVING A LEGACY

*Now that I am old and gray, do not
abandon me, O God. Let me proclaim your
power to this new generation, your mighty
miracles to all who come after me.*

PSALM 71:18

Every man should occasionally turn off the TV to
get a sober hold on reality, and there is no better way
to do this than to stroll through a cemetery. Since
mortality occurs in 100 percent of the male popula-
tion, it's good to be reminded that we spend a very
short time on this earth.

But thanks to Jesus, death is not the end of the
story. Our lives on earth can still speak volumes to
those who come after us. The cold, hard headstone
need not be the only memorial of our existence.

The church of St. Michael's in Lyndhurst, England,

dates back hundreds of years. At one point, the cemetery around the church fell into disrepair, and headstones were broken and scattered. Then church leaders repositioned the headstones as steps along the footpath leading up the hill to the church. In this way, all who go to worship there are assisted by those who have gone before them.

How can the memory of your life aid others in their eternal climb? Concern yourself more with character than comfort. Don't go to the grave with your best work still in you. Strive to give more than you take. Use your time wisely. Center your life on God and His Word. In doing so, you will proclaim God's power to the next generation, and you will leave a lasting legacy of His work in your life.

BOTTOM LINE

Start living and leaving your future legacy today. If you haven't done so already, prayerfully create a life plan that can help keep you focused.

MOMENT OF STRENGTH

Hebrews 11:1-4

ACCEPTING OUR LIMITATIONS

*The LORD is like a father to his children,
tender and compassionate to those who
fear him. For he knows how weak we
are; he remembers we are only dust.*

PSALM 103:13-14

The pressures we face as men are enormous and can sometimes be overwhelming. Most of us are expected to balance the often competing roles of husband, father, provider, disciple, and friend. The expectations concerning our performance in each of these roles can reach a kind of merciless perfectionism that leaves us intolerant and harshly judgmental of anything less than what we consider our very best. We burn ourselves out because there is always something that needs to be done or needs to be done better.

As great as it might be to live a life without any limits, it simply cannot be done. Thankfully, God has no trouble remembering that "we are only dust." He has compassion on us in our limited human capacity. Though we often forget this basic fact of our creation, God has a way of constantly reminding us that we are needy and that we can't make it on our own.

Rather than attempting to deny our limitations, we must learn to accept that we are His creation and that He has a long history of working with those who have limited resources. How is God reminding you of your complete dependence on Him today? Recognizing our weakness is actually a great blessing. It's much better to live according to reality than to deny the truth and exhaust ourselves attempting to do more and be more than God has intended.

BOTTOM LINE

Our limitations are not a surprise to God. Ask Him to help you learn how to accept your limitations and rest in Him.

MOMENT OF STRENGTH

Psalm 46:10

KNOWING PEACE

*May grace and peace be multiplied
to you through the knowledge of
God and of Jesus our Lord.*

2 PETER 1:2, CSB

Peace is talked about throughout Scripture, but how real is it in our lives? Where's the peace when we're at odds with our boss or our spouse, or when we're dealing with a job loss or serious illness? It's easy to get confused, discouraged, or anxious if we're expecting God to deliver us from pain and hardship. That's because He doesn't give us peace as the world gives (John 14:27). In fact, Jesus tells us to take up our crosses and follow Him (Matthew 16:24), which seems contradictory to an easy and comfortable notion of peace.

There's nothing wrong with wanting stability and prosperity in our lives, but we misinterpret Scripture when we claim those as promises from God. Consider that the apostle Paul's life was filled with shipwrecks, beatings, imprisonment, and betrayal (2 Corinthians 11:23-28); yet he apparently experienced peace, and he encourages us to do the same (Philippians 4:6-7). God's peace isn't about our circumstances; it's about being aligned with His will and understanding how He wants to use our circumstances for His glory. It involves a choice on our part to trust God and follow Jesus.

The key is knowing Jesus personally. This comes through intentional and consistent time in His Word, heartfelt prayer, and obedience to what we know He wants of us.

BOTTOM LINE

Perhaps you've seen the following bumper sticker: "No Jesus = No Peace. Know Jesus = Know Peace." That invitation is extended to us moment by moment.

MOMENT OF STRENGTH

Isaiah 26:3

THE NEED FOR REAL FRIENDS

*Jonathan made David reaffirm his
vow of friendship again, for Jonathan
loved David as he loved himself.*

1 SAMUEL 20:17

Every pilot needs a wingman. Every camper needs
a buddy. Batman had Robin. The Lone Ranger had
Tonto. Butch Cassidy had the Sundance Kid. Two
are better than one. Survival in this world is tough—
whether the challenge is physical, mental, emotional,
or spiritual. You need someone to help you along the
tough road ahead.

Never go into battle alone. You don't need a lot
of money or equipment, but you do need a friend.

A real friend walks in when everyone else walks
out, brings out the best in you, doesn't think you've

done a permanent job when you make a fool of yourself, knows you as you are, understands where you have been, accepts who you've become, and gently challenges you to become better.

Do you have someone like that in your life? Someone like Jonathan was for David and David was for Jonathan? They were real friends. They were buddies. They needed each other. They stood beside each other. These men demonstrated mutual acceptance despite differing backgrounds. Promise, not performance, characterized their friendship. Jonathan did not have to do favors for David, and David wasn't expected to kill more giants to remain Jonathan's friend. Their friendship reached a depth of intimacy and trust that few relationships experience.

Who's your Jonathan?

BOTTOM LINE

We need friends for a healthy, happy life.
Without them, we sentence ourselves
to less than the best. Seek good friends,
and seek to be a good friend.

MOMENT OF STRENGTH

Proverbs 27:10

FOCUS OF A FOLLOWER

*Run with endurance the race
God has set before us.*

HEBREWS 12:1

The guys were eager to get to the hunting lodge for a weekend in the woods. Eric and Shawn were the two drivers, with Eric in the lead because Shawn didn't know the way. Everything was going great until Shawn got caught up in a conversation with one of his passengers and didn't notice that Eric was taking the off-ramp to a different highway. After driving for miles trying to "catch up," Shawn finally had to admit he was lost and pulled over to call Eric on his cell phone.

When we're headed somewhere and don't know

the way, we must pay close attention to our leader or we may never reach our goal. Spiritually, it is imperative that we keep our eyes on the one we're following—Jesus. Remember the story of Peter walking on water? When Peter wanted to do what Jesus was doing, Jesus told him, "Come" (Matthew 14:29, CSB). The minute Peter took his eyes off Jesus and looked at the water, he began to sink.

To make sure we stay on the right spiritual path, we have to recognize Jesus by knowing Him through His Word, by keeping our eyes and hearts focused intently on Him, and by avoiding all the distractions and pitfalls that could get us off the path. We're in a race, and the only way to run well is to keep our eyes fixed on Jesus.

BOTTOM LINE

Focus on Jesus so your life will
stay on the right path.

MOMENT OF STRENGTH

Matthew 14:22-33

MONEY, MONEY, MONEY

*Wherever your treasure is, there the
desires of your heart will also be.*

MATTHEW 6:21

Learning how to manage money can be one of the
biggest challenges we face as adults. Day after day,
month after month, questions arise about how to
be good stewards of what we have. We wonder how
much money is enough, what our priorities should
be, and how much we should give to the church.

Struggling to stay solvent can become a routine
part of life. Pay a little bit extra on this bill this month,
then some on the next one next month. There may be
enough to cover everything for the time being, but not
much left over. There are regular expenses that we can

predict, but then there always seem to be unexpected costs that come up.

Cutting back does not necessarily mean having to cut certain things out entirely. The movie you once impulsively purchased on DVD for $20, you now watch on OnDemand for $4. You used to eat out all the time, with barely a second thought to the cost. Now, you savor a once-a-week opportunity for a night out with your family.

It's all about being a good steward. There's a big difference between living in extravagance and simple contentment, and an even bigger one between comfort and poverty. What many of us think of as hardship is a life of unimaginable luxury for millions around the world. Be wise with what you've been given, and be thankful for it!

BOTTOM LINE

Making ends meet can be hard, so pray for
the wisdom to set your priorities correctly.

MOMENT OF STRENGTH

Philippians 4:11-13

CHOICES

*I have given you the choice between life and
death, between blessings and curses. Now I
call on heaven and earth to witness the choice
you make. Oh, that you would choose life, so
that you and your descendants might live! You
can make this choice by loving the LORD your
God, obeying him, and committing yourself
firmly to him. This is the key to your life.*

DEUTERONOMY 30:19-20

What are some of the right choices you've made?
The girl you married? Disciplining and requiring
respect from your children? Staying in a lower-
paying job because it was best for your family? What
rewarding consequences our right decisions bring!

Have you ever made any wrong choices? Taking
a promotion you knew would keep you away from
your family more without seeking God's will about
it first? Experimenting with drinking or drugs as a
teenager? Of course, those are big choices, but what
about the choices we face daily—saying hurtful

words in anger, staying in addictive lifestyles, or cheating on our expense account at work? Bad consequences will follow.

Look at the choices made by Joseph and David in the Bible. In Genesis 39, Joseph flees from the advances of his employer's wife. He later gains greater power and position because of his integrity. On the other hand, David commits adultery, and that terrible choice spirals down into deception and murder (2 Samuel 11). He pays a huge price in the end.

As today's Scripture advises, God gives us choices that have monumental consequences. It's up to us to make the right choices—integrity and character at home, at work, and in our walk with the Lord. There is nothing better than the joy and peace that come from obeying God.

BOTTOM LINE

Resolve today to prayerfully seek
God's wisdom and guidance
regarding every choice you face.

MOMENT OF STRENGTH

Genesis 39:1-19

THE GRACE OF GIVING

You know the generous grace of our Lord Jesus Christ. Though he was rich, yet for your sakes he became poor, so that by his poverty he could make you rich.

2 CORINTHIANS 8:9

Radical generosity is contagious. When others give sacrificially, it can inspire us to do the same, especially when they have less than we do. In 2 Corinthians 8, the apostle Paul is urging the Corinthian church to contribute to a fund-raising project for the Jerusalem church. In motivating them to give, Paul doesn't use guilt or manipulation. He simply tells a story. He calls attention to the generosity of a tiny group of believers in Macedonia who are dirt-poor. He even mentions that he tried to persuade them to keep their money, knowing that they needed it more than those in

Jerusalem. However, they considered contributing to God's Kingdom work a privilege, even when living in extreme poverty.

What would inspire a group of people living in poverty to give beyond their ability? The answer: *grace*. The grace of Christ turns our understanding of the world upside down. It's easy to think you get more by grasping, but in the Kingdom, more comes through giving. The way that God wins the hearts of sinners isn't through guilt and fear but through generosity. In Jesus, God gives beyond our expectations. In Jesus, He broke the bank. He gave all that He had. The more we give, the more we participate in the life of God. The reason we can hold our material resources loosely is that, through Jesus, we have an endless supply of heavenly riches.

BOTTOM LINE

The motivation for giving generously,
even in the midst of scarcity, is the
grace of Jesus Christ. Ask Him to help
you give from a generous heart.

MOMENT OF STRENGTH

2 Corinthians 8:1-15

THE FAITH REQUIREMENT

*There was a man in Jerusalem
whose name was Simeon. This man
was righteous and devout.*

LUKE 2:25, CSB

Too often we want God's resources, but we don't want His timing. We want His presence, but we don't want His patience. We are amateurs at waiting, yet we must wait. God is working. Waiting means we give God the benefit of the doubt and trust that He knows what He's doing.

Simeon must have wondered whether God would be true to His word. He had been promised to see the Messiah, but he was running out of years. His life was at the eleventh hour. God must have reminded him: "Your job is to trust . . . to wait . . .

to accept My timing. That is all. You keep your heart right; I'll keep My promise."

Maybe you're at a point in your life when you wonder whether God will come through. Maybe you are about to give up hope that He will show up. Maybe you feel that time is passing you by. Maybe you want to run ahead of God. Maybe you want to give up on God.

The story of Simeon teaches us that God proves Himself faithful even when it seems as if nothing is happening. His timing is perfect. Our part is to trust—a confident, disciplined, patient waiting for His help and deliverance. God seeks to reveal Himself to us. He wants to meet us. And He will, but it will be on His timetable and in His way. So relax and trust, rather than worry and fret.

BOTTOM LINE

Are you waiting on God or are you
running ahead of Him? He can be
trusted. He is faithful. He will come
through. Choose to wait patiently.

MOMENT OF STRENGTH

Psalm 9:10

WE NEED OTHERS

*Confess your sins to each other and pray
for each other so that you may be healed.*

JAMES 5:16

Mark was terrified. For as long as he could remember, he had pretended to have it all together and had hidden his secrets behind a mask of spiritual activity: teaching Sunday school, leading a men's Bible study, and serving as a deacon. But his perfectionism had worn him out, and he was tired of the facade. Today he was going to come clean and tell his small group about his struggle with pornography and his recent emotional affair.

Instead of rejecting him or throwing him out of the group as he had feared they might, each man embraced him and told him how much they respected his courage. Mark was shocked as the other men began to open up about their own struggles and failures. It quickly turned into one of the most intimate and meaningful meetings they had experienced in years.

Like Mark, we often strive to be the kind of men who are self-sufficient and do not need the help of others, including God. Like Mark, we pretend to be strong. But this individualism has severe consequences. We are left to face our fears and insecurities alone. We were not designed to live isolated, self-sufficient lives. We need each other and were designed for authentic community.

In what ways are you hiding behind a mask of spiritual activity? Are you experiencing real community with other men?

BOTTOM LINE

God wants to bring us to a place where
we can accept our need for others.

MOMENT OF STRENGTH

Proverbs 15.22

WHAT'S NEXT?

For the LORD God is our sun and our shield. He gives us grace and glory. The LORD will withhold no good thing from those who do what is right.

PSALM 84:11

Every man has a special interest in *something*. For some, it's sports—be it baseball, football, hockey, or NASCAR. Other men hunt and fish. It might be a particular book that's a real page-turner, or maybe it's something as simple as a night out with your wife or quiet time at home with the family.

One of the most fun things in life is to be looking forward to something. There's a keen sense of anticipation that for a lot of folks is like being a kid at Christmas again. For the briefest of moments, such eager expectation can be a great escape from the everyday pressures of living in today's busy world, which is filled with responsibilities and stress.

As enjoyable as our interests may be, however, they pale in comparison to our ultimate hope in Jesus Christ. A day is coming when we will stand face-to-face with Him, free from the trials and pains of this world. No more sleepless nights, sickness, or suffering. No more regret or longing.

Let that soak in for a few moments. Our hobbies are fun, yes, but in the end, they're only temporary. A thousand years from now, it simply won't matter how the Steelers did this year or how many home runs you hit in your church softball league. The hope of eternal life with Jesus puts everything in perspective. If we lose sight of that, we will try to get more out of our hobbies than they can provide.

BOTTOM LINE

Our interests can be a lot of fun, but the enjoyment we find in them will be nothing compared to the day we meet Jesus face-to-face. Put your hope in that.

MOMENT OF STRENGTH

Psalm 84

ABOUT WALK THRU THE BIBLE

Walk Thru the Bible ignites passion for God's Word through innovative live events, inspiring biblical resources, and a global impact that changes lives worldwide . . . including yours.

Known for innovative methods and high-quality resources, we serve the whole body of Christ across denominational, cultural, and national lines. We partner with the local church worldwide to fulfill its mission, communicating the truths of God's Word in a way that makes the Bible readily accessible to anyone. Through our strong global network, we are strategically positioned to address the church's greatest need: developing mature, committed, and spiritually reproducing believers.

Our live events and small group curricula are taught in more than 50 languages by more than 80,000 people in more than 130 countries. More than 100 million devotionals have been packaged into daily magazines, books, and other publications that reach over five million people each year.

Wherever you are on your journey, we can help.

Walk Thru the Bible
www.walkthru.org
1.800.361.6131